I0438341

Questions Every Black Person Should Ask

AT LEAST

Once

D.W. Harris

Illustrations by Butch Berry and Ted W.

authorHOUSE®

AuthorHouse™
1663 Liberty Drive, Suite 200
Bloomington, IN 47403
www.authorhouse.com
Phone: 1-800-839-8640

First published by AuthorHouse 7/11/2008

ISBN: 978-1-4343-8086-9 (sc)

Printed in the United States of America
Bloomington, Indiana

This book is printed on acid-free paper.

To my Mom, my little brother, my heart

& the next generation

Just Because Someone Has To Ask...

1. Why do Black people discriminate against other Black people, as if we don't already have enough to deal with?

2. Why can't wealthy Black athletes pool their money together to create something bigger than 15 bedroom houses?

3. What is preventing talented and wealthy Black filmmakers from joining forces in order to create the very movies they complain that Hollywood won't make?

4. Why aren't we sharing knowledge, opportunity, wisdom, love—well, why aren't we sharing with each other, period?

5. Why are we killing off our creativity and imagination because of our desire to make fast money?

6. Why is the desire to make fast money preventing us from pursuing pragmatic and profitable ventures that naturally take time?

7. Who said that we need to make money so fast anyhow?

8. Why have we not understood that helping each other helps uplift us all?

9. Why are Black people still blind to the fact that our individual actions do, unfortunately, represent the whole?

10. Why are darker skin people, from Aborigines to Black Hispanics and Black North Africans, catching Hell all over the world?

11. Why is dark Black skin acceptable only if you have 'good' hair?

12. Why do we still compliment each other on having 'good hair', and will even go so far as to track down the source of the 'good hair' in our family tree?

13. Why is the Black family sold and packaged as a dark skin father, a light skin mother, two biracial looking girls, and a medium to dark skin Black boy?

14. Since the future of Black America is in Black American youth, when will the authors who write about the problems in Black America write books that Black youth will read and can understand?

15. Why do we call Bill Cosby an elitist for saying what people are too insecure to admit is the truth?

16. Did the Black community and sense of community begin to deteriorate when integration started?

17. Why are we still pulling ourselves up by the bootstraps after over 400 years of slavery when immigrants fresh off the boat can turn nothing into something within two generations or less?

18. How depressing was it to learn that some of the more famous Black inventors were not the 'first' to invent their creations—or didn't you know?[1]

1 Taggart, Ian. "Black Invention Myths." June 2008.
http://www33.brinkster.com/iiiii/inventions/

19. Do we think about how the world would be different if Malcolm or Biko or Lumumba or King were not assassinated?

20. Why don't we hold each other accountable for making our neighborhoods look better? I mean, not just saying it, but actually doing it?

21. Is it true that every Black person in the universe has some sort of race related drama in his/her work place?

22. Why are Black scientists the most incognito group of people on the planet?

23. While plenty of Black scientists have excelled in their field, where are the Blacks scientists who have actually INVENTED something that revolutionized their field?

24. When will people realize that racist attitudes do not only loom in the South?

25. Why are you buying your kids the clothes and shoes that gangster rappers advertise if you hate their lyrics and music so much?

26. Why don't we feel obligated to tell our fellow brothers and sisters when they're living wrong? Is it our responsibility?

27. Can we really be mad at the young males for equating guns with respect since America has always glorified men with guns[2]?

2 Katz, Jackson. "Advertising and the Construction of Violent White Masculinity." Gender, Race, and Class in Media. Ed. Gail Dines and Jean M. Humez. Thousand Oaks, CA: Sage Publications, 2003. 349–359.

28. Why do Black women spend whole days in the beauty shop just to get a perm--the same perm that isn't making our hair grow any longer no matter how many natural West African oils we put in it?

29. What happened to the whole Kinté cloth and Black unity movement we had in the early 90's?

30. Why does it seem like the Black people who wear Kinté cloth and talk about African unity today are really creepy or really fake or just really 'deep'?

31. Why are there so many fast food joints in Black neighborhoods?

32. When will people realize that $100,000 Hummers are meant for wars, not for WalMart parking lots?

33. Who said that we need 4 TV's and a Playstation in our SUVs, as if we're traveling the nation on a 6-week concert tour, or turning our car into a bomb shelter?

34. Where is the sense in buying car rims and wheels that costs more than the car?

35. Why must Black people be forced to use that annoying nasally 'Corporate Voice' in order to sound intelligent? (you know what I mean)

36. Are news reporters really going out of their way to interview the most ignorant and embarrassing Black folks on the scene, or does it just seem like it?

37. How obvious is it that Africana people are in a state of emergency when we call well-mannered Black people 'oreos' and suggest the more ignorant Blacks of 'acting their color'?

38. Is Tupac's legacy on Black people and our culture more positive or negative?

39. Even if research did somehow prove that Jesus, Shakespeare, Cleopatra, the ancient Egyptians, and the original philosophers were all Black, would the current state of Black people and our problems really change?

40. How are temporary layoffs and keeping our heads above water 'Good Times'?

41. Not to kick up dust, but has Whitney Houston received her Young 'Un 'legendary' status from Oprah yet? Just curious.

42. How many people know that you can't complain about how awful something is if you're going to turn around and patronize that awful thing every week?

43. How big of a whammy is it to be Black, female, lesbian, disabled, uneducated, and poor? No offense.

44. Are Black people becoming the minority in minority programs?

AFTER ALL THE INTENSE TANNING, THE BREAST AND BUTT IMPLANTS, LIP INJECTIONS AND CORNROWS, HEATHER SUDDENLY FELT SHE WENT "TOO BLACK."

45. What is the image of Black Americans compared to others in the African Diaspora?

46. Why do grocery store chains put their fancy grocery stores with the fresh produce and meat on the wealthy side of town and leave the grocery stores with the fly-infested produce and '2-days until green' meat in the poor neighborhoods — and have the nerve to still charge the same prices, if not more?

47. Why have other races or ethnic groups used criminal organizations like mafias or mobs to monopolize and oligopolize whole industries while Black people use our illegal drug money to become rappers—-who still have to answer to 'tha' man'?

48. Why are Black people in corporate America so afraid to say 'hi' to each other?????

49. Why are we content with Mexicans and Jews and Russians and Asians and everybody else creating businesses in our neighborhoods?

50. Since Black hair care is a billion dollar business, where are all of the Black-owned beauty supply stores and beauty products?

51. Why do we wallow on how many racist bank loan officers will tell us 'no' when all we need is one to say 'yes'?

52. Is anyone else concerned that major companies feel they need to use hip hop culture in order to market to the Black consumer? I mean, you do notice the 'superfly' Black person who does the hip hop dances in the soda and car commercials?

53. On second thought, why are Black people letting themselves be so easily targeted by stereotypes, and yet, we have the nerve to complain about how racism just isn't going away?

54. Who told Black people that it's better to spend money on things that depreciate than it is to have financial investments or equity in a house?

55. Why have we fallen into this notion that a French, Italian, Belgian, English, or generally European anything is better than what we can make?

56. Why can't more Black heavyweights at investment banks and financial institutions help their brothers and sisters out with free financial advice?

57. Well, would our brothers and sisters even go to the meetings to listen to the free financial advice that the Black heavyweights at investment banks and financial institutions should give?

58. Are we scared of investing in financial markets?

59. Or, are we so busy catching up on our bills that we don't even have the money to invest in financial markets?

60. Does the answer to the above have something to do with the fact that we've become a community of consumers instead of capitalists?

61. If a global economy is most beneficial to those countries and people who have something to contribute to the global marketplace, where does that leave Black America and Africa?

62. Why are we struggling to save jobs that will eventually move to China and India, instead of taking the steps to be trained for more competitive and higher paying jobs?

63. After their accent elimination classes, will my friends in India and China take all of our jobs?

64. Should we hold Black senior execs at ad companies accountable for creating socially responsible images of Black people?

65. Has anyone noticed that when there is a majority of Black folk working in one area or department, the majority of management personnel for that department and the company are non-Black folk?

66. Are those companies simply overlooking qualified Blacks, or are qualified Blacks far and few between?

67. How did substandard service at Black businesses and universities somehow become the norm, and the butt of our own jokes?

68. Can we diversify our investments to more than sports teams, clothes, clubs, and food?

69. Why do we spend money on ridiculously expensive things in order to impress people who are just as broke as we are, and furthermore, people who we don't even like?

70. Have the IMF and World Bank made any progress in helping the depressed economies of countries?

71. Have capitalism and the American Dream taught us to justify being greedy as well as why we shouldn't feel obligated to help those who have less?

72. How many credit cards do Black families have compared to our White counterparts?

73. How much credit card debt do Black families have compared to our White counterparts?

74. Now compare the above to how much you have invested in a place where your money is earning interest?

75. How much did your television cost?

ENTERTAINMENT

76. What's so bad about having a Black doctor and lawyer on TV when we should be aspiring to those professions in order to buy all the material stuff with which we're taught to be so obsessed?

77. Why don't we think about winning an Oscar for anything other than acting?

78. Is it just me, or are videos on the country music channel about 10 times less expensive and 10 times more creative and classy than the 'bootyshake on a lowrider' videos?

79. When will the fools who bring guns and knives to our concerts and award shows realize that if they can't leave the house without a gun or knife then they probably shouldn't be leaving their house at all?

80. Why are there one thousand rappers all claiming to be #1 in any given hour?

81. Would an alien that just landed on Earth think that Black people are sex-crazed animals who can't use English correctly if it looked at BET for one hour?

82. What is the overall message of a channel that devotes twenty three hours to glorifying rich and successful Black rappers and sport stars, and only one hour telling Black youths that they don't have to be rap stars or play sports in order to be successful?

83. When will we get tired of playing the omniscient Black sidekick or the comic relief role in TV shows and movies? Better yet, since we've mastered the 'Black people rising over discrimination' movies, can we diversify into political thrillers, and actions, and epic adventures now?

84. Should we look at White actors playing Black/Biracial characters as just another acting job, or as one more acting job taken away from bona fide Black actors?

85. What does it mean when Black males feel they need to rap about murder, sex, big money, and drugs in order to make it-- forget the fact that more and more come from middle class parents who pay for them to go to prep schools in the suburbs[3]?

86. Is it a good thing that R&B singers are trying to carve out a piece of the contemporary gospel music pie? Or, weren't you paying attention?

3 *Hip Hop: Beyond Beats and Rhymes*. Prod./Dir. Byron Hurt. *DVD. Media Education Foundation. 2000.*

87. What in the hell is going on with Lauren Hill? An objective question, of course.

88.How did getting a record deal suddenly become the ultimate aspiration?

89. Shouldn't the people responsible for choosing the celebrities to be in these 'help the community' campaigns at least make sure that their chosen celebrities aren't doing or glamorizing things that *destroy the community?*

90.Why is it that Black filmmakers who make one or two excellent films soon fade into oblivion?

91.Why do bail bond companies now know to target Black radio stations for their next potential customers?

92. Is anyone else upset about the lack of Black dramas (that have nothing to do with a Black man running from the law or selling drugs) in the theaters or on TV—or has anyone noticed?

93. Would it matter how much TV we watch or don't watch if the rest of our priorities straight?

94. Not that racial stereotypes can't be true or funny, but need the bulk of our jokes revolve around race-based humor?

95. When will rappers rap about how to do math or science, or anything that might actually help young people?

96. Need we go through the trouble of making independent movies if we're going to create the same characters and plots that Hollywood can make on a bigger budget?

97. How many Black Americans know who Robert Jones or Nina Simone is?

EDUCATION

"Glory, the Ghetto Fairy" says ...

98. Why is *The Diary of Ann Frank* required classroom reading, but no one ever bothers to mention anything about reading the slave narratives?

99. Isn't it time to muster up the courage to ask whether our kids do worse than their peers in school because we might not be doing something right as parents?

100. Why do we know European history from front to back but pause in silence if someone asks us about Great Zimbabwe, the Ashanti Empire, or Kush?

101. Have you ever asked yourself why McDonald's is so much more committed to teaching us about Black history (during February) than our own schools?

102. Does your answer have anything to do with Economics--considering the number of McDonald's found in or around our neighborhoods?

103. Why will we jeopardize our entire future just to be cool for a few folks who won't even remember our name 3 years after graduation?

104. Why do schools talk about the same four or five Black Civil Rights Leaders and the same four or five Black Abolitionists during Black History month, as if Black history is summarized solely by the American Civil Rights Movement and Slavery?

105. Do we encourage our kids with action in addition to words?

106. Is the answer to better teachers and better schools really summarized by higher taxes? I.e. where in the heck is our money going right now? Is it being used effectively?

107. Are our kids really prepared for college once we go through all of the trouble to get them there?

108. Why do we have to give our kids prizes or money for bringing home A's, as if that behavior should be anything less than ordinary?

109. Do you know whether your child is doing her Black music history report on Ciara or Marian Anderson?

110. And who is this teacher who will let your kid get away with writing a Black music history report on Ciara, and why in the world is he/she still teaching?

111. Why are Black people scared to be nerds, as if being an idiot is going to get us any place?

112. Before cursing the teacher out, might we consider that our kid really did break the school rules?

113. Can someone please create an initiative to get more Black men in college so that higher educated Black women can have someone to date?

114. Not that rapping and athletics aren't promising career opportunities, but what about academic achievement as an option for getting out of the ghetto?

115. When will our HBCUs have an academic reputation that matches or supersedes their reputation for having the best-dessed students?

116. Do Black people who like to read nonfiction and watch the Science Channel ever feel lonely?

117. If you've been saying 'I'm going back to school one day' for ten years, isn't it time you ask, 'What is stopping me?' or, quite frankly, 'Why do I keep lying to myself?'

118. How many Black parents stay involved in their children's education--post-elementary?

119. Why don't we know our children's teachers' names until one has to call home with a bad report?

120. Will the growing digital divide send us back to being 'tha help'?

121. Why the heck do we buy $200 Nike and Reebok cross-trainers and basketball shoes when our kids are simply going to school? I mean, do cushiony soles help them get to the classroom any faster?

122. What happens to the Talented Tenth after they graduate from the Harvards and Yales?

123. How many Black descendants of American slaves are there in the Black Ivy League now anyway?

POLITICS

124. How much faith are we to have in *Ebony*'s top ten list of Black leaders if it makes a new top ten list every week?

125. Can we thank Barack Obama for saving us from this trend of having to call our Black community leaders Rev. So and So?

126. And since Obama is our new great leader, does it now mean that all Black people are forbidden from saying anything negative or critical about him?

127. Oh, yes. And with all of the success that Obama has had, does this make it easier for White people to now say that there is no racism in America?

128. Do we realize that White (and Black) people are becoming more frustrated with affirmative action and quota programs, and how that will effect us in the future?

129. Does being Black mean that we're obliged to vote for and/or support a person because he/she is also Black?

130. How about we not consider every Black person of influence or authority as the leader of all the Black folk?

131. Assuming we do get reparations, which is---hmm, anyway,
assuming we do get reparations,
what we do with it?

132. Why don't we become
our own role models and
leaders instead of waiting
around for *Ebony* to tell us
who they should be?

133. Will Black people hold
the Democratic Party more
accountable for protecting our
interests, especially if we're going to act like it's our only political alternative?

134. Are the 'circumstanc-
es' surrounding Hurricane
Katrina (both years before
and days after) the perfect
case study for negligent
homicide against the fed-
eral government?

135. When exactly shall Black people overcome?

136. Don't we all know someone who has truly been on welfare forever and counting?

137. How many people know that self-sufficiency is better than a hand out?

138. Why are the Black people who come up with ridiculous, off-the-wall conspiracy theories to explain our current conditions called 'deep' instead of 'crazy'?

139. How unified need we be before it becomes okay to start helping each other?

140. Isn't a commitment to uplift our brothers and sisters in every way all the unification that we really need anyhow?

141. Is anyone else upset at Louisiana Rep. William Jefferson for his scandal--not because of his own graft, but because he is (well, supposedly) also collaborating with other corrupt African business and political leaders?

142. And couldn't Rep. Jefferson have done something sophisticated with the money, like Jason Bourne or, better yet, like every other corrupt political leader in the world? You know, put the money in a cool Swiss bank account instead of wrapping it in aluminum foil and hiding it in his freezer as if a pound of chicken??

143. Do any of us have goals of becoming a U.S. Ambassador to an African country?

144. Does Black America know what our NAACP is doing these days?

LIL' KIM DOES A PSA.

RELATIONSHIPS

145. Why are Black women still waiting on their perfect Black man if he's not waiting on you?

146. What does it mean when heterosexual men have to take lessons from homosexual men on how to be better men for women?

147. Does the media make an extra effort to spotlight Black athletes who have non-Black wives or girlfriends, or does it just seem like it?

148. Can we stop our zoological-like fascination with the "DL brother" and get on with brainstorming ideas of how to celebrate their coming out parties?

149. Is the Black family heading towards extinction?

150. Isn't it sad that we now have to be 'proud' of Black men for choosing a Black woman, especially if he has been to graduate school?

151. Have you ever asked yourself what legacy are you leaving for yourself or your children?

152. Why do we recognize how beautiful and valuable our African culture and products are only after White people have sold it back to us?

153. Why is it that nearly everyone except Africans owns the precious minerals and resources that come from Africa?

154. Since Oprah has opened the door, can we ask other Black entrepreneurs to invest in the development of African people and African businesses?

155. Is it not amazing and self-fulfilling to go to Africa and witness a whole government and country being run by Black folks—and no one finds it out of the ordinary? Beautiful.

156. Can we stop defining Africa as a place where only wild animals and famished, war-torn people live, and begin to also highlight the beautiful people, places, and cultures found there?

157. Is anyone else excited about the development of Nollywood and the growing self-reliant African film industry?

158. Why are rich countries ex-pecting poor African nations to pay back billions of dollars in loans when those countries could better use their money for education and job creation—if corrupt officials don't pocket the money first?

159. Will someone create a petition to get the Soweto choir and Teddy Afro and P-Square and Souleymane Diamanka and other great Black world artists some airtime on our so-called Black Entertainment Television channel?

RELIGION

160. Why are more Christians becoming mirrors of the TV and radio stations they listen to, i.e. becoming religious only on Sunday, 5-11am?

161. What is the use of having so many churches crowding every corner of our most depressed neighborhoods if the churches aren't going to make any real impact on the communities surrounding them?

162. Is it kosher to ask whether the biggest Black churches in America are being built primarily by the support of the Black female demographic?

163. Speaking of religion, has anyone noticed that the more educated you become, the less religious you seem to become? What up with that?

164. Are any of us still blaming our own lack of initiative and slave mentality on the biblical curse of Ham?

165. Why are there more women leading their families to church if men are supposed to the be spiritual heads of the house?

166. Why do gangster rappers thank God after winning an award as if God had something to do with song lyrics that go against 99.9% of everything that almost every religions' God says to do?

167. Don't Muslims seem a heck of lot more disciplined than Christians?

168. For that matter, don't many Hindus, Buddhists, Confucians, Agnostics, and even Atheists seem a heck of a lot more disciplined than Christians?

169. If you pray to God for a job, but you never actually fill out any job applications, should you be surprised if your prayer is never answered?

170. Isn't it great to see celebrities using their social influence to help out in the AIDS awareness initiative[4]?

171. In the same breath, isn't it a bit sad that we need a celebrity to convince us to do that which we should already be humanly compelled to do?

172. If we saw the real pictures of human illness and disease, would they have a bigger impact on our behavior or would we just turn away like we usually do?

4 *GAP, Inc. 'RED' Advertisement initiative*

173. Why are African-Americans (and African-American women in particular) lagging so far behind in the AIDS prevention front[5]?

174. Black Americans, are we really still fighting lead poisoning[6]? The big initiative from the early '80s??

175. If average Americans can't afford to buy medication and we have the highest per capita income in the world, what makes pharmaceutical companies think that people in poorer countries can?

5 CDC. "Fact Sheet: HIV/AIDS among African Americans." June 2007. DHHS, Center for Disease Control and Prevention. June 2008. <http://www.cdc.gov/hiv/topics/aa/resources/factsheets/aa.htm>
6 Dines, Kaylyn Kendall. "UMDNJ Resources Say Age, Race, and Season are Factors in Vitamin D Deficiency and Lead Poisoning." May 8, 2007. University of Medicine and Dentistry of New Jersey. June 2008. http://www.umdnj.edu/about/news_events/releases/07/r050807_Age_Race_and_Season.htm

176. When will we start getting our mentally ill real medical help instead of ignoring their conditions or sending them to rural towns to live with our grandparents?

177. Is the fear of sweating out a perm the #1 reason why Black women don't exercise more?

SUPER BLACK WOMAN'S OTHER KRYPTONITE...WATER!

178.Shouldn't we all be aware of our personal risk to Diabetes?

179.Would soul food really be so bad if we did the physical activity that we're missing in the first place?

180. How many people are going to close this book and never think twice about making any adjustments in their behavior or thinking—and will still have the nerve to wonder why nothing is changing?

181. Am I a hater?

After Words

Everyone who has made it this far should feel more than compelled to discuss their answers with others, or to provoke others to ask themselves these same questions or derivatives thereof.

While I tried to infuse humor in topics that, I feel, are rather depressing and shameful, the foremost purpose of this book is to officially open the door to self-assessment. Quite frankly, I created this book out of my own grave concern for the community of which I am apart. Some might call me a Generation X'er or an MTV/BET generation kid who doesn't know what she's talking about, but considering my youth, I feel like I can give a perspective of the Black community and Black youth that many do not often hear. Contrary to how most Blacks in my generation are packaged and marketed, there are pockets of us who are sincerely and deeply concerned about the direction of our community, and one need not only dress in hip hop clothes and/or use slang in order to get our attention.

I personally became so overwhelmed with questions, based on general observation and dreadful statistics that I honestly felt myself becoming hopeless—-and I didn't want to be. After having the same discussions with friends and family time after time about 'why things are like this' and 'why things are like that', I could hear their own hopelessness and cynicism and mounting indifference. I, too, longed to simply be free of my desire to care, like a good many of my peers and many before us. Still, I cannot help but mention how similar our concerns were, and how many of us wanted to see things changed. We didn't like the way we were being portrayed on TV and in movies. We could see and feel the shortage of Black men in colleges and universities; We knew the discomfort of being the only Black person in the room and having to defend Black interests; We knew the awkwardness of having to explain how 'all Blacks are not like—that.' Conversation after conversation, and what would happen? Obviously, nothing happens when you're preaching to the choir, and that's what we were doing for the most part. Even more, how many of us who took the time to preach to the choir were actually DOING something? Not many, not even me.

We are all so good at debating about theory and history and policy, but when it comes to actually putting necks out on the line, very few are found. How many Black people do you know who are enlisting in the Peace Corps? How many Black people do you know who are using their JD's, MD's, MFA's, or PhD's to help us? How many Black creative types do you know who are using their creativity to shape a richer view of Black culture and the African Diaspora? Perhaps, I'm a victim of my own limited exposure, but I have to admit that I don't see very many of our wealthy and powerful fighting to preserve our culture and creativity. Of course, there are exceptions, wonderful exceptions, but what is the rule? And are we helping to perpetuate that rule, that standard? I see far too many of the rich and powerful hoarding their power and money, as if somehow they can take it with them to their graves. A bigger question to ask—how much of their wealth lasts beyond a generation or two generations? I see far too many of us who are willing to regurgitate instead of create and experiment, i.e. take risks. And I find that disheartening. Yet and still, something inside of me can also understand that point of view. I like the idea of making fast money as well. However, I believe the real choice of whether to follow through with our own individuality or take the easy route reflects back on where we'd like to see our place in history. For the Black community, that choice seems to be whether to make a few dollars today or to a have a legacy that reaches into tomorrow. It's simply a choice between the short run and the long run. We can most certainly live for the short run, but for Black people, the unfortunate question is if we even have a place in the long run, and if so, where is it?

Over the years it seems to my untrained eye that Black people have become so comfortable with stereotypes of ourselves that we've actually aided in their prevalence. Too often we cave in to the status quo, mumbling of little choice when, in fact, there is always a choice. Either we participate, or we do not. Either we pay to see ignorant depictions of ourselves, or we do not. We can always walk away from money; we do not have to support ignorance; we can always say 'no'. We do not have to be forced to change our stories or ourselves to appease others. And by doing so, we force the 'market' to conform to us instead of us always conforming to the marketplace. Think of the power of the Civil Rights boycotts. Too many of us are not willing to take risks today, and therefore, little changes. We simply must take more risks. But today, instead of fighting for equality, we need to fight for our future, a healthy future. We've become so indifferent about our second and increasingly third tier place in various societies that we no longer question the blatantly harmful images and statistics that act to define us. In essence, many stereotypes have become normalized and now float through the air as the inferential racism that we (well, some of us) complain about. Bottom line: there is always an option.

As more and more of our older generations pass away, I wonder if the spirit of community and hope for betterment that they witnessed before the Civil Rights Movement will also pass away. Today, there seems to be a dangerous illusion that Black people are doing so well on our own that there is little need for community. Just as it is in the world around us, emphasis is placed on individual success—at all costs. Forget the repercussions, most especially if they do not happen in the short run, or in a time or space in which we might be a/effected. My point of view is that we need to change that manner of thinking.

As a descendant of American slaves, I can't help but to take a moment to speak to us directly. No, we might not be picking cotton anymore, but many of us have become captive to the American Dream, working so hard to gain an inkling of economic mobility that we forget about the wellbeing of our kids. We forget to instill in them values of hard work and the importance of education. Immigrants, and first and second generation Black people who arrive in American communities mobilize and form support groups among themselves. Finding themselves in a new place, they share wealth, knowledge, resources. But where are the descendants of American slaves? Are so comfortable in our new home that instead of supporting each other, sharing with each other, we compete, forgetting the value of community, forgetting that we are a part of the same community? Of course, Black people are as different from one another as there are shades of Black, but let's not forget our shared experiences. I asked one young Black gentleman, maybe 25 or 26 years old, for help, and his response: "I've spent a year amassing all of these resources that I have. You go out there and do the same that I did." Of course, he said this without thinking of the ineffectiveness of several people repeating the same movements. If one person advances, pass on the information so that others do not have to repeat. Instead of repeating, we can move higher, together. What can a bitter community or people do, besides stagnate? Mentalities like this are what we need to rectify. My hope is to see the descendants of slaves as owners of million dollar businesses, the future leaders of our cities, our government, in our nation's best colleges, and one day, the leader of our country--this country that we helped to build.

Some of us give up too easily on our brothers and sisters who've become trapped in hopelessness. The key to uplifting all of us is not to give up on people who might have given up on themselves. On the contrary, the key is to exert hope and demonstrate alternatives. We have to start expecting more from ourselves, and more from those around us. And as long as we allow stereotypes to dominate the perception of who we are to others, we are all victims--no matter what neighborhood we try to escape to. Stereotypes do not discriminate.

I believe that when we can find the meaning in self-dignity, integrity, self-respect, and did I mention integrity, we will and can go farther than any other movement. This concept doesn't limit itself to a finding faith movement, wiping out illiteracy movement, teaching men to be fathers movement, teaching women to be mothers movement, getting out of debt movement, blue and red love movement, and whatever other programs people come up with. Respect for self, for family, and for community are at the core of advancement.

In closing, I wish for Black people to come out of this mindset in which we berate each other for telling the truth about each other. Talking honestly about OUR OWN faults without constantly being on the defensive or feeling like a Benedict Arnold is the first step that we can take towards moving forward. What progress occurs if we can't even be honest with ourselves? What progress can occur if we're in a perpetual state of denial? Most importantly, when do we start taking responsibility for our own mishaps? After all, the race card can only be played so many times before it runs out. And we're damn near overdue.

D.W. Harris